I Have a Skeleton

by Simone T. Ribke

Content Consultant

Catherine A. Dennis, N.P.

Reading Consultant

Jeanne M. Clidas, Ph.D.
Reading Specialist

Children's Press®
An Imprint of Scholastic Inc.

Library of Congress Cataloging-in-Publication Data
Ribke, Simone T., author.
I have a skeleton/by Simone T. Ribke.
    pages cm. — (Rookie read about health)
Summary: "Introduces the reader to the human skeleton"— Provided by publisher.
Includes index.
ISBN 978-0-531-22703-9 (library binding) — ISBN 978-0-531-22579-0 (pbk.)
    1. Skeleton—Juvenile literature. 2. Human anatomy—Juvenile literature. I. Title.
II. Series: Rookie read-about health.
QM101.R48 2016
    611.71—dc23   2015021121

Produced by Spooky Cheetah Press
Design by Keith Plechaty

© 2016 by Scholastic Inc.

All rights reserved. Published in 2016 by Children's Press, an imprint of Scholastic Inc.

Printed in China 62

SCHOLASTIC, CHILDREN'S PRESS, ROOKIE READ-ABOUT®, and associated logos
are trademarks and/or registered trademarks of Scholastic Inc.

1 2 3 4 5 6 7 8 9 10 R 25 24 23 22 21 20 19 18 17 16

Photographs ©: cover: D. Roberts/Science Source; 3 top left: Catherine Ledner/
Getty Images; 3 top right: Potapov Alexander/Shutterstock, Inc.; 3 bottom:
ryby/iStockphoto; 4: Joe Drivas/Getty Images; 7: D. Roberts/Science Source;
11 background: iStockFinland/iStockphoto; 11 girl: AlexandraFlorian/Thinkstock; 11
skeleton: pixologicstudio/iStockphoto; 12 boy: BJI/Getty Images; 12 x-ray: Nick
Veasey/Getty Images; 15 girl: fishwork/iStockphoto; 15 x-ray: Nick Veasey/Getty
Images; 16 girl: Lane Oatey/Getty Images; 16 skeleton: Chris Harvey/Shutterstock,
Inc.; 19 boy: Olga Solovei/Getty Images; 19 x-ray: Nick Veasey/Getty Images; 20
girl: aabejon/iStockphoto; 20 x-ray: Nick Veasey/Getty Images; 23 girl: Catherine
Ledner/Getty Images; 23 x-ray: Nick Veasey/Getty Images; 24 feet: ryby/
iStockphoto; 24 x-ray: thailoei92/Shutterstock, Inc.; 27: anytka/iStockphoto; 28 top
left: salez/iStockphoto; 28 top right: ryby/iStockphoto; 28 bottom: vita khorzhevska/
Shutterstock, Inc.; 29: Jamie Grill/Media Bakery; 30: Christopher Futcher/
iStockphoto; 31 top: salez/iStockphoto; 31 center top: Springer Medizin/Science
Source; 31 bottom: DWithers/iStockphoto.

Illustrations by Jeffrey Chandler/Art Gecko Studios!

Table of Contents

What Is a Skeleton?

Are you floppy like a jellyfish? Can you squeeze into small places like an octopus?

Did you answer "no" to these questions? That is because you have a skeleton!

FAST FACT!

An animal that has a skeleton is called a vertebrate (VER-tuh-brayt).

A skeleton is a part of your body. It is under your skin. It is made up of a lot of bones. Some bones are very small and others are very large. All bones play an important role, no matter their size.

FAST FACT!

Doctors use an X-ray machine to see the bones in our bodies. The image made by the machine is called an X-ray.

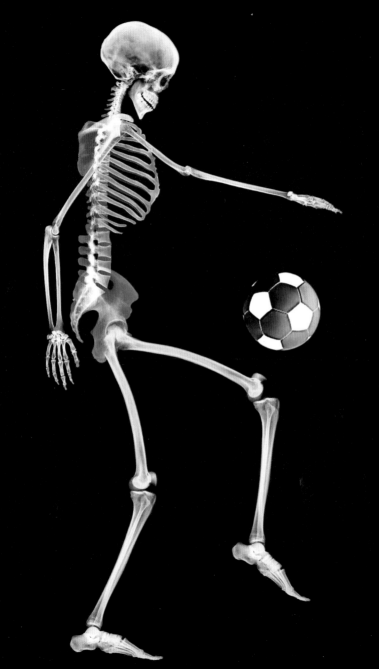

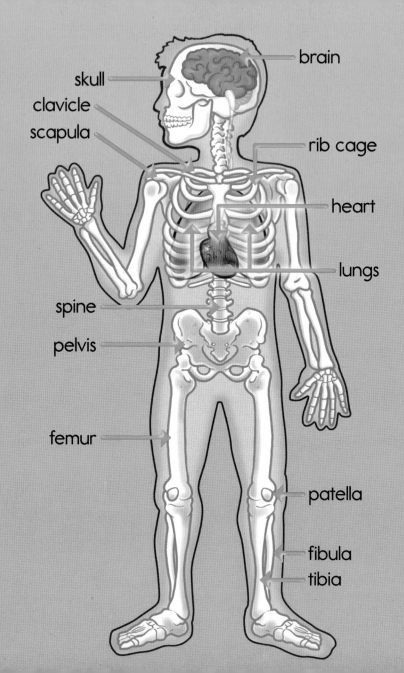

brain

skull

clavicle

scapula

rib cage

heart

lungs

spine

pelvis

femur

patella

fibula

tibia

Your skeleton holds your body upright. It also protects your body's **organs**. For example, your skull protects your brain. Your ribs protect your heart and lungs.

This diagram shows the names of some bones in your skeleton and some of your organs.

Heads Up!

The skull is at the very top of your skeleton. It is made up of 22 bones. One of them is the jawbone.
The jawbone is also called the mandible. It is the only bone in the skull that is able to move. It moves when you talk or eat.

skull

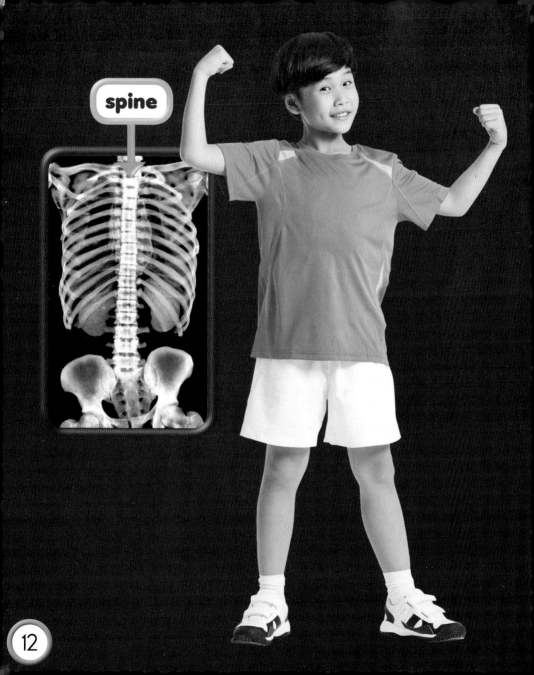

spine

Your spine starts at the bottom of your skull. It goes all the way down your back. It supports your head and lets you stand up. It also lets you bend and twist. The spine is made up of 33 small bones called **vertebrae**. Seven of these are in your neck.

FAST FACT!

The spine ends in a point called the tailbone. If you had a tail, this is where it would be!

What's in the Middle?

Most people have 12 pairs of ribs. They are attached to the spine in the back. Seven pairs are attached to the sternum in front. This is the flat area over the heart. The next three pairs are attached to the other ribs in front. The lowest pairs do not connect to anything in front. The ribs and sternum are called the rib cage.

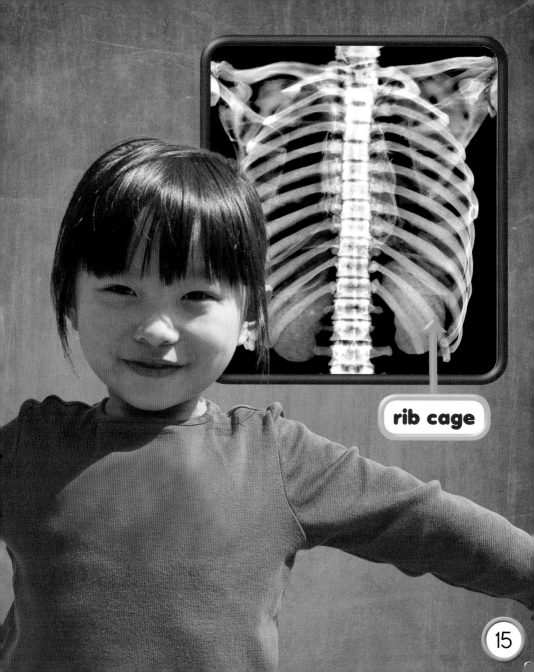

rib cage

scapula

clavicle

16

The pectoral girdle supports your shoulders and arms. It is made up of four bones: two clavicles (KLA-vih-kuhls) and two scapulae (SKA-pyoo-lie). There is one of each on each side. You can feel your clavicles below your neck. You can feel your scapulae on your back below your shoulders. Each scapula has a triangle shape.

FAST FACT!

Bones can have more than one name.
A clavicle is also called a collarbone.
A scapula is also called a shoulder blade.

You have three bones in your arm. There are eight bones in your wrist. There are 19 in your hand. Special tissues connect your arm bones to your shoulders. They are called **ligaments**. They are a lot like rubber bands. They make it possible for you to move and bend. Ligaments help form a joint. That is where two bones join together.

FAST FACT!

Your wrist allows you to wave and twist your hand.

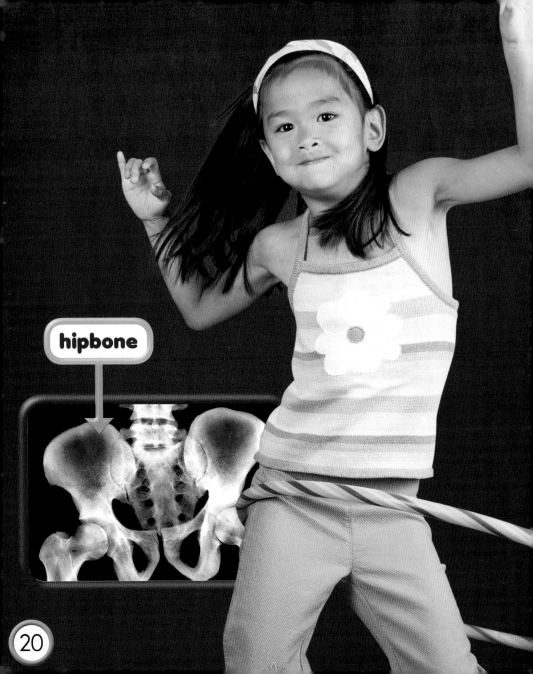

hipbone

The Movers and Shakers

Your pelvis supports your legs. It is made up of two hipbones. There is one for each hip. Strong ligaments connect the tops of your legs to your hips.

FAST FACT!

The hip joint is made of a ball and socket. The rounded end of one bone fits into the cuplike end of the other bone. That lets you move your legs to the front and back, up and down, and side to side.

There are four bones in each of your legs. The thighbone is called the femur (FEE-muhr). It connects to your hips. The tibia (TIH-bee-uh) and the fibula (FIH-byuh-luh) connect to your femur at the knee joint. The fibula is also known as the shinbone. Your kneecap is a bone called the patella (puh-TELL-uh).

FAST FACT!

The femur is the largest and heaviest bone in the body.

femur

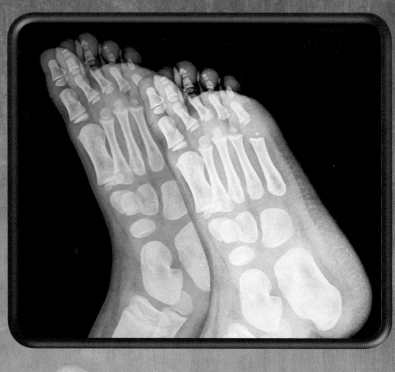

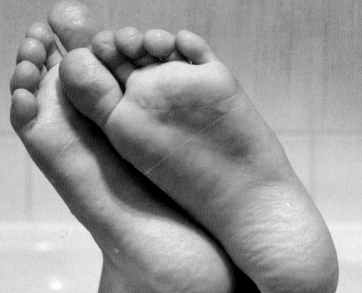

Your foot attaches to your leg at the ankle joint. There are 26 bones in your foot and ankle. There are 33 joints in your foot. Does that seem like a lot of bones and joints for one foot? That is because your feet have a lot of important jobs. They help you stand upright. They also let you walk and run.

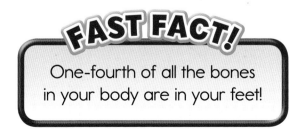

FAST FACT!

One-fourth of all the bones in your body are in your feet!

Each joint in your skeleton has **cartilage**. This body tissue is hard yet bendable. Cartilage in the joints keeps the bones from touching each other. It is very painful when joint bones touch! Cartilage also helps the different parts of your skeleton move.

Isn't it incredible to think of everything that goes on beneath your skin? Your skeleton helps you do amazing things!

Your nose and ears are also made of cartilage.

Look at the pictures below. Which of these body parts is *not* made of bone?

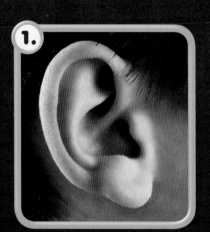

1.

2.

3.

Answer: 1.

Explore Your Joints!

1. Your hip joints and shoulder joints are similar. How many different ways can you move your leg? How many different ways can you move your arm? How is this similar to the way your leg moves? How is it different?

2. Your knee and elbow joints are also similar. How many different ways can you bend your leg? How many different ways can you bend your arm? How is this similar to the way your leg bends? How is it different?

How are your elbow and knee movements different from your hip and shoulder movements? How are they similar?

Strange but True!

Who do you think has more bones, babies or adults? The answer is babies! Adults have only 206 bones. Newborn babies have about 300! As a baby grows, some of his or her "extra" bones fuse together. That means two or more bones grow together to form one big bone.

Just for Fun

Q: Which bone is the most musical?

A: The trom-bone!

Q: What do you call a skeleton that does not want to work?

A: Lazybones!

Glossary

cartilage (KAR-tuh-lij): strong, bendable material in some parts of the body (such as the nose and ear) and some joints

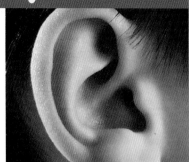

ligaments (LIG-uh-muhnts): tough bands of tissue that connect bones

organs (OR-guns): parts of the body, such as the heart and the lungs, that do specific jobs

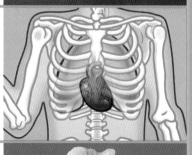

vertebrae (VUR-tuh-bray): the small bones that make up the spine

Index

Facts for Now

Visit this Scholastic Web site for more information on the skeleton:
www.factsfornow.scholastic.com
Enter the keyword **Skeleton**

About the Author

Simone T. Ribke writes children's books and educational materials. She is also an artist. Simone lives with her husband, children, and schnauzer in Maryland.